Core Strength for Peace

. . . exercises for the workplace, marketplace, school, and home

by

Tobie Hewitt

Spiral Path Press

ISBN-10: 1467916064
ISBN-13: 978-1467916066

My deepest thanks to the following people who in one way or another encouraged me on this path:

Patti Borrelli, William Claire, Tina DeSouza, Rich Johnson, and Kitty Moran

. . .

Dedicated to Mom and Jane,
and
to William, who dreams of peace . . .
for everyone

TABLE OF CONTENTS

Preface

The original title of this little book was *Core Strength for the Workplace*. I was witnessing the frustrations and challenges of working in an atmosphere that while being predominantly pleasant and nurturing also fostered a "better than"/"lesser than" environment. Those with less power often seemed beset by the demands of those with more. Rather than drawing on inner resources to realize that the circumstances of immediate need were temporary, I saw individuals reacting with tension, anxiety, frustration, and a victim-mentality, rather than drawing on the idea that we are all one working toward a common goal (both in terms of corporate goals <u>and</u> universal goals). At the same time, I realized that the people instigating the tension had no idea (in most cases) of their effect on others. In other words, the oneness of the work community, understood through a solid foundation of spiritual core strength, was lacking. We had resources we were not utilizing—we lacked the tools and abilities to find peace within ourselves and between each other—we were acting and reacting from a foundation of fear and spiritual core weakness.

What, I pondered, could strengthen our spiritual core strength so that we could overcome that fear? What could we do as individuals to change ourselves into centered, peaceful, loving beings, ready and able to interact with others in a like manner, from a calm and nurturing perspective?

The path to core strength laid itself out before me as an obvious methodology—(1) begin with meditation to become aware that there actually is a spiritual core that can be strengthened with practice; (2) release stress, which will allow the gathering and centering of energy that will fill the space created when stress is released; (3) utilize this energy to grow the awareness of the connection between the individual spirit and the universal spiritual reality; and (4) utilize this spiritual core strength to build community and peace.

Meditation helps us to find the calm space within ourselves and to strengthen it, which in turn allows us to grow our awareness of, and utilize our internal energy in a productive rather than destructive manner, both as individuals and in the larger community. Increased mindfulness—in each moment developing an awareness of being and the state of that being, without thought or judgment—helps us to foster an ability to act and react from a perspective of focused calm.

Practicing releasing stress allows us to release momentary fear and frustration and to thus act and react from a peaceful perspective, unhindered by negative, unproductive energy. Normally, stress is a part of the "fight or flight" instinct that our early ancestors needed to survive. While being confronted by an angry or demanding coworker, friend, or family member can feel sometimes like being faced with a hungry tiger, we are not normally at risk of loss of life or limb. When we allow stress and fear to be our reaction to the hostility of others, they have control over our intrinsic being; they can reach into our core and manipulate our ability to think, feel, and act/react. A far healthier mode of being than that of stress would be to take a deep breath, center our spiritual core, and react from a space of calm awareness.

From this centered space, and with calm awareness, we can become aware that we are all imbued with individual expressions of the larger spiritual reality, which helps us to interact with others as we would like others to interact with us. At the core of most of the world's religions and spiritual paths is some form of the Golden Rule, that we should treat others as we would ourselves like to be treated. In doing so, we can recognize that we are all imbued with spirit and that that spirit is our essential self, and, further, that we are individual expressions of the larger spiritual reality that is the creative force in the universe.

Finally, with our spiritual core strengthened through meditation, stress release, and awareness, we can actualize the potentiality that we are all, in fact, one community, able to live in peace and harmony. By utilizing the lessons learned by strengthening our spiritual core strength, we can alter our intra- and interpersonal communications methods, allowing for a new paradigm in which fear, distrust, and inequity are replaced by oneness and peace. Thus, in this atmosphere, we are able to find productive, rather than destructive, solutions to those challenges that might otherwise divide us.

As I continued working on this book, I realized the idea of spiritual rather than physical core strength was growing, as world events continued to instill fear, violence, retribution, confusion, enmity, and all sorts of negative, lower vibration behaviors. By utilizing the simple lessons presented in *Core Strength for Peace*, I hope that you will find the peace within to hear the call to create peace in the world.

Introduction

What is Core Strength?

Core Strength for Peace presents ideas on how to acknowledge and strengthen one's inner energy center to achieve a more peaceful and harmonious internal, home, work, and world environment. Through instruction and exercises, readers will become aware of tools they can utilize to cope with otherwise stressful situations in their life.

What is your physical core? What does it do?

Physical core strength is important for the general health of the physical body. Strong core muscles—those in your trunk, your abdomen, pelvis, back, etc.—help to maintain a strong back, good posture, healthy weight, etc. If allowed to become weak and flaccid through non-use, the body suffers from a variety of maladies, including backache, balance issues, and ailments that impede the natural movements of the body while putting strain on joints and ligaments throughout.

When core muscles are toned and functioning well, physical core strength is achieved, which allows you to move and act in a stable and centered manner as you engage in activities including walking, playing, and even sitting quietly.

How can it be strengthened?

Core muscles can be strengthened through exercises such as those done on a stability ball.

What is the spiritual core? What does it do?

Your spiritual core is an energy center located within the physical core that permits the awareness and expression of empathy, compassion, and insight. It is the essence of who you are within your physical reality.

Just as a strong physical core allows your muscles to act in harmony, so does a strong spiritual core permit you to act harmoniously within yourself and with others. A weak energy center leaves you susceptible to a diminished self-awareness and, by extension, poor awareness and comprehension of external factors and influences. Like physical core weakness, spiritual core weakness can leave you open to pain and distress to both your physical and spiritual selves. Becoming aware of and strengthening this energy center can strengthen self in larger dynamic situations (relationships/family, friends, co-workers, companies, countries, world).

How can it be strengthened?

Through meditation, stress reduction, spirit awareness, and practicing intra- and interpersonal communications methods, Core Strength for Peace can be achieved. By developing this inner strength, you will gain a space of inner peace from which it will be easier to deal with the stressful situations that tend to arise in the various environments in which you find yourself. In addition, you will gain the ability to concentrate in a manner that widens your perspective of short- and long-term tasks (e.g., increasing out-of-the-box thinking and acting). Also, as you become more centered and aware of your spirit, there is the possibility that "coincidences" will occur more frequently. Pay attention to these . . . when you become more in tune with your self and its role in the universe, you will start to get help along the path you are traveling through this life.

Techniques for developing Core Strength for Peace:

Locate and develop your energy source (i.e., meditation)
Gather and center your energy source (i.e., stress reduction)
Practice The Namaste Response (i.e., spirit awareness)
Change your perspective and, in turn, change the paradigm (i.e., intra- and interpersonal communications methods)

Developing Core Strength for Peace

It is easier to be a spiritual creature in a calm, nurturing setting than in the middle of a busy intersection waiting for a light to turn and traffic to clear, in a crowded conference room during a long presentation, when dealing with unruly children, in a neighborhood with a perpetual lawn mower buzzing early on a Saturday morning, in a store filled with rude customers and workers, or in any number of situations in which others are not fulfilling our personal need for peace. At times like these, it is important to be able to find the spiritual core strength within us to help us deal with that which we cannot change but which we can respond to in an optimally peaceful and beneficial manner.

Meditation—Locate and Develop Your Energy Source

Many people believe meditation is difficult, or at least believe they do not have the patience or concentration to meditate. Actually, meditation may take no more than a minute, although for serious practitioners, meditation can last for an hour or more.

Meditation is also called mindfulness, though this can also be considered a larger, minute-to-minute state of being—an awareness of being present in the moment you are in, rather than projecting your thoughts backward or forward in time. Meditation provides an internal environment for what is known as "being here now." When we learn to be cognizant of our own internal workings and how to access our calm state of being, we are able to take it to the street and to the marketplace, giving us a peaceful internal place from which to experience the world around us and in which to react to any and all situations as they arise.

Meditation is known to increase concentration and promote feelings of peace and centeredness. Through meditation, you can learn to control your responses (physical and mental) to stressful situations. Meditation allows you to connect your internal energy to a larger energy source, giving you a sense of feeling both grounded and supported at the same time.

While the benefits of meditation are numerous, practicing meditation to develop core strength will increase your ability to focus and to quickly employ techniques to bypass stress. This will give you a peaceful space in which you can maintain your serenity when others are losing theirs and/or striving mightily to get you to lose yours.

There are many forms of meditation and each person should find the one he or she is most comfortable with. Presented here are techniques that can be accessed anywhere and anytime and are easily accomplished in a few quiet (or maybe not so quiet) moments. Mastering simple meditation techniques provides us with the first steps towards developing our core strength for both internal and external peace.

Conscious Breathing:

Conscious breathing is based on becoming aware of your breath. Just as your breath is important when building physical core strength (breathing out when exerting and in when releasing), so too is breath important when building mental/spiritual core strength.

Sit, stand, or lie tall, spine erect, but not strained, head relaxed, an extension of the spine. Think of a cord running from the top of your head through the ceiling, up to the sky, and into the cosmos holding you comfortably erect (if lying down, think of the end of the cord comfortably reaching through the wall, out of doors, past the city buildings, and into a peaceful meadow. Also, think of a cord coming out of your feet and, again, through the wall, the city, and into another meadow). If sitting or standing, feel a cord running from your feet, through the floor, into the ground under the building, and into the earth. Bottom line—feel your tallness (no matter how short you are) and know that the earth supports you and the sky will keep you tall.

Gently close your eyes and gently breathe in through your nose, keeping your face muscles and lips relaxed. Relax your tongue and gently rest it on the roof of your mouth, behind your front teeth or wherever is comfortable for you. Remember, the goal is to establish focused relaxation, not to perfect a pose or set of rules. Feel the breath fill your core (gently—don't force the breath down, but, rather, let it naturally enter your lungs and feel these expand. When you sense that the breath has completed its inward path, allow the breath to flow out through your nostrils, naturally, without force. In none of this should you strain. This is a natural, peaceful breath. The only difference is your awareness of the process and not straining. This is not the fight-or-flight breathing associated with tension, animosity, or stress—in other words, this is stress-free breathing. Now comes the "hard" part—silently count your breaths on the intake. Four breaths is a good number. Feel the air entering through each nostril, flowing into the back of your mouth (keep your throat muscles relaxed), and allow the breath to naturally flow into the core. Now, each time you breathe in, silently count—first breath is "one." Second breath is "two." Third breath is "three." Fourth breath is "four." And then begin again. It should take about a minute to complete all four breaths. Don't think of anything but the breath going in and the breath going out. If counting is too distracting, just breathe. Keep your mind peaceful and silent, just focus on breathing. After one or two cycles (four breaths each), you should feel calmer and more in control, if not of the situation, then of your reaction to the situation.

Om/Word/Mantra Meditation:

While still breathing consciously (or at least in and out), you can repeat (in your head or softly aloud) a word or mantra that has meaning for you and helps to bring you to a place of peace and mental/spiritual core strength.

Mantras are words or phrases, which often find their origins in Sanskrit. Examples would include "om mani padme hum" (roughly translated as "hail the jewel in the lotus") or "jai guru deva om" (which means: "glory to the shining remover of darkness"—which can be found in the Beatles "Across the Universe") or my favorite, "Om namah Shivaya ("I honor the divinity within myself" or "I honor that which I am capable of becoming" or "I bow to the higher nature of my inner self.")

The use of mantras is a nice meditation style because while the words have a meaning that is important to be aware of, and which can help to guide you to a more serene and enlightened state of being, you can derive the benefits by thoughtfully intoning the sounds of the words over and over, imparting a sense of serenity that has been found in them by many people for centuries. In a sense this practice connects you to a larger peaceful reality while you are seeking your own inner peace.

Repeating "Om" or "Aum" is similar to using a phrase as indicated above. The difference is you are focusing on this one word and intoning it, without force or discomfort, for the duration of your outward breath. "Om" has no meaning such as the mantras have, but instead is the sound believed to be that of the universe, the sound that permeates everything. When we practice meditation by intoning "Om" we are tapping into a vibrational reality that surrounds us and is in us. As such, the use of "Om" as a meditation tool can serve to connect our core to the universal core. "Om" not only connects us to something larger than ourselves, its very vibration echoing within our being can instill a sense of calm awareness. A minute of breathing and intoning "Om" can help to center calm energy within your core.

Another form of word/sound based meditation may be more accessible for some, and that is simply repeating a word that is meaningful to you. "Peace," "love," "calm," or any other word that when you think or say it fills you with a sense of tranquil joy. Simply say or think the word as you breathe.

A helpful tool for sound/word/mantra meditation is a mala. A mala is a set of beads, either in necklace form (108 beads) or bracelet form (27 beads—27 x 4 = 108). In whatever form the mala takes, there is one bead—the guru bead—that is larger than the rest and allows you to keep track of when you have completed the number of mantras you wish to repeat. One hundred and eight beads is considered a sacred number in the Buddhist and Hindu religions. In an extended meditation form, the mala helps to focus on the mantra or sound while keeping count of the number of times the mantra or sound is being repeated, either aloud or silently. Starting at the bead after the guru bead, you simply allow your fingers to roll through each bead as you repeat your mantra/word. While this may sound time consuming and not at all useful as a quick meditation technique, it actually takes very little time to make a circuit around the necklace or bracelet. While a mala is not necessary for meditation and some may find it a distraction, it can help further focus the mind as you work towards Core Strength for Peace.

Happy Place Meditation:

An easy and instantaneous meditation method, and one that can be practiced anywhere, is what I call "happy place meditation." As the name implies, in this meditation you journey in your mind to a place—real or imaginary—that you find calm and peaceful. My personal favorite is Crater Lake in Oregon. I find the deep blue lake and natural surroundings ideal for happy place meditation. While practicing conscious breathing, I simply start visualizing Crater Lake, trying to make the image in my mind as real as possible. This technique is perfect for when you need a quick mental vacation from the situation in which you find yourself. I find it especially useful in the dentist's chair! If you have trouble visualizing your happy place, you can always keep with you a small picture of the place that you can focus on. Whether practiced in your mind or while contemplating an external image, this is an especially accessible method of meditation.

I have focused on meditation as our first step to Core Strength for Peace for several reasons: not only does meditation promote a sense of calm and well-being within an individual whenever it is utilized, these techniques also have the ability to foster a course of action in opposition to the normal fight-or-flight reaction we so often find ourselves experiencing in stressful situations. If we have tools that can help us remain calm, focused, and centered in these situations, we will be able to react to them from a peaceful, rather than adversarial or victim mentality. Practicing meditation techniques will strengthen your energy core while connecting you to a larger reality, one undergirded by the same oneness embodied by the sound of "Om." Entering into this larger community through meditation can help to build a wider sense of peace than that of simply one individual.

You may have noticed that all of these meditations help you get centered through breathing. Breathing connects us to each other, to the planet, and to the past. As we breathe we are in-spiring that which is necessary to sustain life and, at the same time, breathing in the oxygen created by the trees and plants around us. We become connected to the whole of being and, in doing so, can find our center and place of peace. Breathing connects us to each other and in addition connects us to all time and space. We are here in this moment in time, at this place in space, and it is our breath, more than anything else, that can help us realize our relationship to everything around us, in a sense helping us to realize our oneness with everything.

To find our center in this is to find the source of our being. Finding this center strengthens our core. This often feels like an expansion within us, radiating from between our solar plexus and heart. This fullness of being promotes and supports a peace that helps us to feel calm in the face of apparent chaos, and aware that we are part of a larger, more peaceful whole. It is the feeling of standing solidly and in a relaxed manner and in this feeling, we know that nothing can knock us over. And . . . all of this starts with something that is as simple as a breath.

Working on meditation techniques not only helps strengthen our core so we feel we can handle almost anything, but it also serves as a first step in reducing any stress we may encounter throughout our day. Practicing meditation and stress reduction techniques helps us to find and maintain our individual core strength, which is peaceful in nature. In turn we can share these feelings, rather than those of tension, distrust, misunderstanding, angst, etc., with those around us and even those at a distance.

Stress Reduction—Gather and Center Your Energy Source

Decreasing our stress and increasing our focus helps us to think clearly in any given situation. Even a cleansing breath can help clear the fuzziness from our thinking patterns and put us into a clear space of peace within, in which we can find answers and appropriate responses to situations as these arise. As we prepare to face a new or known stressor, or when trying to overcome nervousness about attempting or creating something new, breathing techniques learned in meditation practice can be further developed to reduce our adrenaline-laden responses to these situations.

The stress reaction, with adrenaline pumping through your veins, may have been the appropriate response when faced with a charging tiger, but it is probably not as useful when sitting in an audio conference when the participants are all fighting for their individual points of view. In such a case, the mute button would provide you with a moment to find the peaceful center within yourself and, from that stance, reenter the conversation/debate.

The stress response to a situation has numerous physical, mental, and emotional manifestations, none of which ultimately will help you accomplish your objective. Physically, stress may lead to high blood pressure, stomach pain, headaches, or obesity. Mentally, stress can impact your ability to think clearly, to make reasonable decisions, to be productive, or to problem solve. Emotionally, stress can cause you to be irritable, anger-filled, depressed, or sad. Stress allows others to manipulate your reactions to situations and can lead you to become hostile and isolated within the work or social group.

When we allow ourselves to be overwhelmed by stress, we open ourselves to manipulation by others, both in our immediate environment and in the world at large. Stress increases our fear response, which in turn creates in us the need to find solutions to the problems that stress makes us feel are insurmountable. In doing so, we may put our trust in others—family members, coworkers, national and international political and religious leaders—who wish to use our fear to their advantage, in other words to have power over us. Stress creates a situation in which we give our personal power away, and allow ourselves to accept as truth anything that promises the alleviation of the discomfort brought on by stress, even when the proffered solutions may cause us harm in the end. If we learn to release stress ourselves, we maintain control over our lives and remove the possibility of losing our sense of self and of our connection with the wider community. Through easy stress reduction techniques we can remain centered, peaceful, and focused, and in turn fortify our spiritual core strength.

Practicing techniques to alleviate the stress response will help you to gather and center positive energy, release negative energy, and allow you to act and react in a positive, calm, and productive manner.

Deep Cleansing Breath:

When we breathe normally, we inhale and exhale in a shallow manner, allowing the air to stay in our chests, rather than allowing it to flow through our core, and fully fill our lungs. This shallow breathing takes no thought and is a physiological necessity to staying alive. It is a few steps above the very shallow fast breathing that occurs in response to stress and fear.

Breathing is fundamental to our continued physical existence. Inhaling provides us with the oxygen vital to our organs; exhaling removes harmful toxins. Furthermore, focusing on our breathing and especially deep breathing encourages us into a state of peace and centered rather than scattered thinking. A deep cleansing breath helps us to avoid snap reactions.

Simply taking a deep belly breath and slowly letting it out is a great way to relieve stress and can be done anywhere, not only in the "quiet" of your cubicle but also walking down a busy street or in rage-filled traffic.

Practicing deep cleansing breathing is easy and immediately rewarding. Close your eyes and breathe in, allowing the breath to fill you deeply and completely. You can place your hands on your stomach or your lower back to experience the feeling of your lungs expanding. Do not force the breath in, but simply breathe deeply and completely. When you are comfortably filled with oxygen, pause for a moment and hold the air within you, then allow the breath to leave your body. This can be done in several beneficial ways. You can simply allow the air to leave via your nose, or you can purse your lips and blow the air out. Experiment with the manner you find most calming. The entire breath should take less than 10 seconds, and you will find that even one such breath will help alleviate stress and allow you to regain (or find) your center.

When practiced daily for a few minutes, you will find that taking a deep cleansing breath in a moment of stress becomes second nature. Deeply inhaling and then blowing out any tension-filled feelings will quickly help you to develop your core strength in order to find the peace within and, eventually, allow you to share your internal peace with the wider community.

Alternate Nostril Breathing:

As the name indicates, alternate nostril breathing (also known as "pranayama," or "breath control") is breathing through one nostril at a time, which helps to focus not only the breath but the mind and spirit as well. In addition, it helps to balance both sides of the brain, allowing us to act and react in a more focused centered manner.

Sit comfortably, and begin with a few calm and cleansing breaths. With your right thumb, gently press against the side of your right nostril, closing off air flow. Breathe in through your left nostril. Using your index finger, close off your left nostril, release your right nostril, and exhale the air through that nostril. Breathe in through the right nostril, close off the air flow with your thumb, release the left nostril, and exhale through that nostril. This completes one full cycle of alternate nostril breathing. Start again with inhaling through the left nostril and complete 5–10 more cycles.

Gather and Center Energy:

Similar to meditation in method, gathering and centering energy is a very focused exercise that anyone can do. Starting with your arms at your sides, raise them slowly with palms upwards while taking a slow, deep breath; bring hands together, palms and fingers touching, and slowly bring your hands down into prayer pose in front of you while slowly exhaling the breath . . . hold this pose and take a few more slow breaths in and out. Repeat the series, this time thinking of your hands gathering energy from around you as your lift them. As you continue the movement into prayer pose, feel this energy between your hands radiating up your arms and into your body, centering in your core right behind where your hands are placed.

Following are diagrams of the arm and hand positions for this exercise.

Starting with your arms at your sides,

raise them slowly with palms upwards while taking a slow, deep breath;

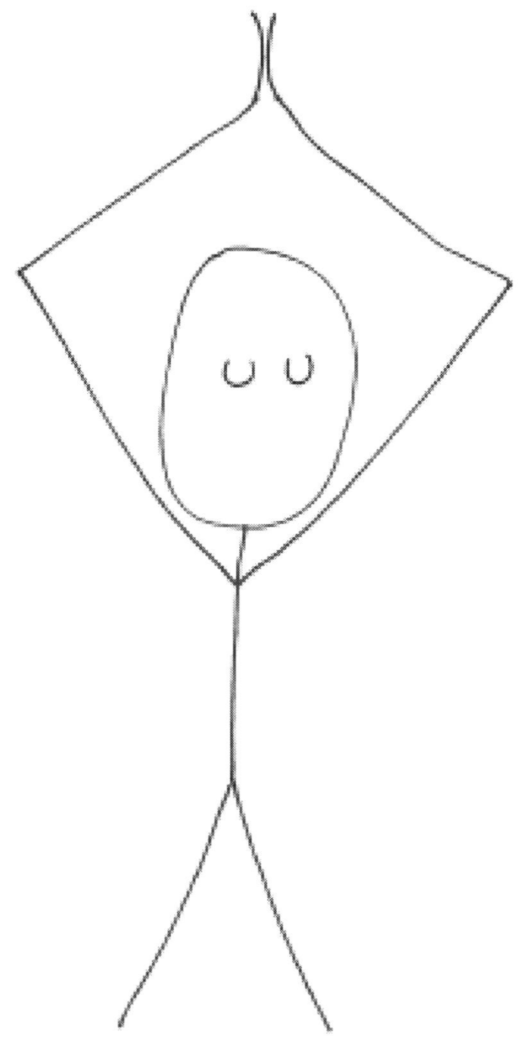

bring hands together, palms and fingers touching,

and slowly bring your hands down into prayer pose in front of you while slowly exhaling the breath . . . hold this pose and take a few more slow breaths in and out.

You can test the existence of this energy by moving your hands slightly apart, about 6 inches. You should begin to feel the energy moving between your hands in the form of heat or a gentle vibration. This energy is the same energy that permeates every atom of the universe and which connects all atoms to each other. It is the energy that sustains and flows within the interdependent web that exists on every plane and dimension. Thus, the energy that you feel during this exercise not only relieves stress but also allows you to experience the vital energy that connects you to everything and everyone in the universe.

This energy is essential to the development of individual core strength, and in turn, to the development of an all-permeating peace.

Muscle Tension Release:

You can also release stress energy through a systematic process known as the muscle tension release technique, which is accomplished by focusing on tensing and then relaxing the different muscles in the body.

This exercise may be best performed when lying down, though you can try it in a sitting position. Starting with your feet, point your toes and tense the entire foot, hold for a moment, and then release. Then, tense your legs, hold, and then release. Continue tensing and then releasing the rest of the body, one section at a time—the stomach and torso muscles, the arms, and the neck (by pulling the chin into the neck). Finally, tense the entire body, hold for a slow in breath and then release. This can be done several times to attain a state of physical relaxation, even when the circumstances around you are anything but relaxed.

Additional Stress Reduction Tools & Techniques:

Exercise is a great method of reducing stress. Walking and running do not require a huge investment of time or money and even twenty minutes can effect a reduction in perceived stress. Lifting weights can have the same benefit as the muscle tension release technique. Exercise can make you feel better about yourself physically, mentally, and emotionally and help you to develop not only physical but spiritual core strength as well, which helps to stave off stress.

A warm, relaxing bath scented with lavender and surrounded by candles is always an optimal stress reliever, but not so useful in your office cubicle.

There are physical objects that you can keep in close proximity that can help to relieve stress, including squeeze balls, mala beads (described in the meditation section), and appropriate crystals. Smoky quartz crystals absorb negative energy and can sit unobtrusively next to your computer keyboard. Holding the crystal when practicing meditation or stress reduction techniques can help draw negative energy from your body and can absorb negative energy that is flowing in the environment. A quick rinse in cool flowing water will discharge the negative energy and allow it to go down the drain. There are many crystals available that will speak to your own spirit, so I recommend a trip to your local gift store that sells crystals. Too new-age for you? Think of crystals as decorations with the added benefit of being psychological tools.

Practicing meditation and stress reduction—centering and gathering your energy source—will help you to gain control over your individual spiritual being. Awareness of the energy that is the essential you through practicing these exercises will increase your spiritual core strength. This awareness will help you on your path of developing connections with others and working towards peaceful coexistence through compassion and empathy.

Spirit Awareness—Practice The Namaste Response

In what I call The Namaste Response, you become aware that the energy you have within you, and which you have been nurturing through meditation and gathering and centering, also exists in all the other people around you. When you practice The Namaste Response, you acknowledge that energy in another person and allow your energies to connect.

> Albert Einstein was fascinated by Mohandas Gandhi. He watched newsreel after newsreel of Gandhi's doings in India. Having seen Gandhi greet people in the street with his hands placed together, as if in prayer, and with a bow, he wondered what Gandhi was saying (newsreels had no sound in those days).
>
> Einstein wrote Gandhi and asked him what he was saying. The simple reply: "Namaste." Einstein then wrote again to ask the meaning of this Hindu word, "Namaste," and the reply was: "I honor the place in you where the entire universe resides. I honor the place in you of light, love, truth, peace and wisdom. I honor the place in you where, when you are in that place, and I am in that place, there is only one of us" (Author/source unknown; http://thefourprecepts.com/propublish//art.php?artid=58).*

Understand that you are filled with various forms of energy. Some of this energy is stored in the muscles to enable you to move and sometimes you find yourself with an excess of this energy, which you can release using the methods described above. Other energy is utilized in your brain, moving ideas around, and helping you to absorb new information, or instructions regarding what you should be doing. The energy in your brain serves many purposes and helps to regulate and monitor the energy throughout the rest of your body. It is like the hard drive of a computer, helping to run all the programs, but the difference is that there are emotional energies blending in and mitigating the human processes.

Then of course there is the energy that you take in, that keeps you warm and nurtures you, that comes from the foods you eat and beverages you drink. The food or beverage contains energy of its own and when you eat that energy, it is incorporated into your energies, and helps you function, move, and think.

While energy can neither be created nor destroyed, the energy that runs the physical body dissipates after the transition known as death. However, there are other energies that exist, which are recognized by those in alternative medical fields such as acupuncture, acupressure, Reiki, etc. That energy is described as centered in seven areas of the body and flows along what are known as meridians, that not only connect these centers, known as chakras, but also flow elsewhere in the body.

There is also another energy, which is what Gandhi and Einstein corresponded about. This energy can also neither be created nor destroyed, but it forms a body separate from the physical body and continues after the physical transition commonly referred to as death. This spiritual energy, which is not bound necessarily by religious belief or dogma, is not only individual, but is also part of a greater whole, both while integrated in the body and also without the necessity of a body. This energy is the same in every living creature. It forms the basis for our common existence on this plane and all others. Maybe this seems a little "out there" for you, but actually, as you sit here reading this, it is more like "in there," i.e., in you.

This energy goes by many names in many different cultures and belief systems, but it is what forms the basis for the idea of The Namaste Response . . . that is, by recognizing that we each possess this energy, this spark of divinity, we can each recognize our common being. Since we all contain this divine spark, this essence that is our spirit, it is a small step to begin to not only recognize each other as spiritual beings, but to use this knowledge to find bases for respect and understanding. It is this, then, that allows us to fully empathize with another, stepping into their shoes, and walking that proverbial mile.

In the home, the marketplace, or the workplace, this knowledge can serve to ease tensions between us and others. If we are indeed connected in this way, then releasing antagonistic feelings and behaviors before these fester seems to be the only choice possible . . . your right hand does not constantly slap at your left hand, trying to force it to do certain things a certain way, but, rather, both hands work together to accomplish a goal, whether it's creating a piece of pottery, cooking dinner, or writing a business plan. The phrase "we are all in this together" takes on a larger meaning when viewed in the light of our interconnectedness, our co-existence in an interdependent web of reality.

Something larger than you is at work here, and it is you—locating, developing, and working from that essence is what spiritual core strength is all about. Developing a strong spiritual core strength and, in turn, an awareness of your part of the whole can help you develop The Namaste Response in your daily life.

Following are some exercises that can help you develop the aspect of spiritual core strength that results in and allows for The Namaste Response.

* There is, apparently, no proof that this exchange actually took place, but it is very nice to think that it could have done so.

Making Energy Connections with Others:

How can we determine for ourselves that this energy exists and how can we practice connecting with others via this energy? One method is to try to reach out to a stranger without that person being aware that it is happening.

This exercise involves going to a location where a variety of people might be gathered, such as the central court of a mall or a busy restaurant. Sit quietly and allow yourself to relax. Take a few deep breaths. Select a person sitting across the way. Do not stare at this person, as that will make him or her uncomfortable. Simply know that this is the person you are going to connect with, then imagine your spirit reaching out to his or her spirit. Try to recognize the essence of you recognizing the essence of that person. You are not trying to be intrusive; you are simply trying to connect on a spiritual level with this other spirit sitting across from you.

Remember, you are not having a stare-down contest with this person. He or she should not be aware that you are reaching out to them (unless, of course, they, too, are trying to connect spiritually with another, and then the connection might be quite immediate and deep . . . connecting with another spirit is a joy-filled and exhilarating experience).

Now, as you reach out to this other person, focusing your awareness both on your spirit and this other person's spirit, you will become aware of a sensation of warmth and perhaps a slight vibration. This sensation will most likely be detected in the area between your solar plexus and your heart. This is the area of the chakras associated with gut instincts, intuition, love, and compassion and it is on this level of love that you are actually communicating with this other person, even if that other person's physical being is not aware of such communication. When you detect that glimmer of love growing within you, then you will be experiencing the bond associated with two spirits interacting. This is not the love of romance novels, but rather a more spiritual love. It is a part of the sensation of oneness with the world around you, with the spirit plane, with the universe.

Detecting a vibration in this part of your body is verification that you are perceiving and connecting with the spirit of another person. It may take a few tries (or trying with different people) to achieve this awareness, but once the connection is made, it is an unmistakable sensation. This exercise will help you not only to connect spiritually with another, but will allow you to become more aware of and more familiar with your own spirit and its reality. Once you feel comfortably at home working with your spirit being, and acknowledging its abilities, you can try to send forth a wave of love to those around you. You may be quite surprised to detect a wave of love coming back at you. Even those around you who are not aware of their own spirits, or are not used to utilizing this part of themselves, contain that essence that is well-aware that another spirit is reaching out towards them with love, and they will respond with a vibration of love sent back to you.

Awareness of “Coincidence” Exercise:

When embarking on the path of developing core strength and its attendant awareness of spiritual realities, it is a good idea to start carrying around a small notebook in which to record your observations about your meditation and stress reduction practices, and also the coincidences and synchronicities that will occur as you further follow your path of development. When you expand your awareness of the energies that are in and around you, coincidences and synchronistic moments happen with greater frequency. Keeping track of these occurrences will give you a solid record of your development, and with time you may be able to discern a pattern that indicates an inherent lesson or message.

What do coincidence and synchronistic moments have to do with The Namaste Response? These moments indicate a connectivity, of yourself with the larger world, and, in proving this reality, can help you to connect with other individuals through acknowledging that their divine spark, their spiritual being is connected to your own.

As you develop your awareness, you will begin to understand that, in reality, there is no such thing as coincidence—everything that appears to be coincidence is actually a purposeful tap on the mind by different aspects of universal consciousness.

The Smile Exercise:

This is an easy exercise to try as you walk through a supermarket or through town. Try smiling at those whose paths you cross. Don't run up to them and force your smile upon them. Just send a polite smile to everyone you encounter. Some people will ignore you, some will give a polite half-smile, and others will flash a full and happy smile your way. Once in a while, you will encounter one who recognizes the connection you are trying to make through the smile and will even go so far as to say "hello!"

Smiling at a fellow human being is another way of saying "Namaste." The spark of the divine in me recognizes and bows to the divine spark in you. Our smiles become the outward manifestation of our inner spirit. In our moment of smiling at each other, we are one.

The awareness that you can make a connection with another through as simple an act as smiling should deepen your acknowledgement that there is a larger energy available to you through which you can connect with others. Strengthening your spiritual core through practicing The Namaste Response helps you connect your spiritual self to the larger energy that flows through the universe. The Namaste Response connects us all as one in the interdependent web of existence.

On the Road:

The man who cuts you off in traffic, the woman who is driving two inches off your rear bumper, the teen driving too close as he or she weaves in and out of traffic at break-neck speed . . . these are your brothers and sisters who are perhaps running late, or trying to get to the hospital before a loved one passes, or are simply distracted and not paying attention. Their intent is not to do you, personally, any harm. They are centered in their brains and monkey minds and not in their spiritual core. Road rage is allowing that physical plane aspect of those people to dictate how you are acting and reacting. Your blood pressure rises, your hands grip the wheel too tightly, and words you would not normally use in polite company come spewing from your mouth. There is another way.

Using The Namaste Response, try this instead. When confronted by fellow drivers who are not acting optimally and safely on the road, ask yourself why they might be doing so. Try to feel compassion and empathy rising within your spiritual core and send a silent message of love and caring to these people. They may not be consciously aware of the positive feelings flowing towards them, and it is highly unlikely that they will immediately change their mode of driving, but somewhere inside of them, their spirit will perceive your kind intention and that seed of divine communion will be planted.

If enough people start sending out thoughts of love to those who act aggressively, the hostility that fills them will begin to ebb and, eventually, flow away. Then, the road that is another path through life on this physical plane will proceed in a spirit of kindness and cooperation.

The Namaste Response, in essence, is recognizing the interconnection between you and others. Practicing feeling connected through mindful expansion of your awareness of self and others is an important step in developing spiritual core strength as a means towards peaceful coexistence. As you travel through your day, imagine radials of loving energy reaching out from you towards others. The more you do so, the more you will find that there are increasing moments when you feel others' loving energy peacefully reaching out to you.

Intra- and Interpersonal Communications—Change Your Perspective and, In Turn, Change the Paradigm

When we all work for the same company or organization, for example, we work in a hierarchy that helps to develop and carry out goals in order for the productivity of the work to serve a common purpose (profit, etc.). In a larger sense, the entire world can be seen to be working for a common goal . . . the evolution of humankind into a peaceful, harmonious unity of being.

One of the aspects of modern life (or perhaps one that has been present throughout history) that works against core strength and The Namaste Response, is the idea that one can only win if someone else loses. While this may be true in the case of situations set up for that sort of competition, such as sports, on a daily basis this reeks of the idea that one needs to claw past others to be on some never attained top (there is always someone higher) in order to be successful, rather than working peaceably toward a common goal where everyone reaps the satisfaction and perhaps rewards of a job well-done and/or accomplished. The "do anything to reach the top" philosophy has a disastrous effect on the workplace and in society, pitting one person against another and leading to all sorts of "better than" mentalities that give rise to poor treatment not only of others but of self, since this way, this path requires excessive energy expenditure, leading to physical, emotional, and spiritual exhaustion. Then there is the karmic consequences of treating others as rungs on a ladder, each to be stepped upon as one climbs higher. When we seek to work cooperatively, in harmony, we not only assure a pleasant path for all, but can rest assured that we are treating others as we would wish to be treated. To try to win at all costs creates a constant adversarial environment that is detrimental to a well-functioning work or home environment and a solid spiritual core.

To diminish someone else is to diminish oneself—since we are all part of the same whole. Sometimes you do run into somebody who wants to run you over—then how does spiritual core strength help you? Sometimes the other person will remain difficult. Your actions, emanating from your core, will give you the insight and strength to do the job with a glad heart. And, by witnessing your core strength, the other person may learn and grow themselves.

Changing your perspective changes the paradigm, no matter the position of the other person.

Following are exercises to help you change your perspective and, in turn, change the paradigm by practicing intra- and interpersonal communications methods.

Metta Meditation:

Metta meditation . . . at any time, in any place chant: "May all beings be peaceful. May all beings be happy. May all beings be safe. May all beings awaken to the light of their true nature. May all beings be free." There are various versions of this, but it serves to draw the individual out of self and into a sense of community with the universe.

You need not chant loudly; chanting softly under your breath or even silently will have the same effect.

11:11 Response:

When we strengthen our spiritual core strength through meditation, the gathering and centering of energy, and becoming aware of our connection to each other, we also awaken to the knowledge that there is an interdependent web of life that supports us and our intentions. This web binds us to each other and asks us to be responsible for all other beings on the planet. One way in which we can work together for the greatest good of all is by heeding the call to participate in group positive thought and intention, what I call 11:11 mindfulness.

11:11 mindfulness manifests as a "coincidental" awareness of 11:11 a.m. or p.m. or any time that ends in 11. Now that you are aware of this, you will find that your awareness is drawn to that time more frequently than simply by chance. The beauty of this is that you are not the only one to whom this is happening; thousands of people in your time zone and around the world are becoming aware of that same time, in that same moment. In that minute, and it only lasts the minute encompassed by :11, those so called (and the number grows each day) focus our intention on sending out healing and love to all who share our planet. Close your eyes for that minute, take a deep breath, and meditate on sending out positive thoughts. You can even recite, silently or aloud, the Metta meditation: "May all beings be peaceful. May all beings be happy. May all beings be safe. May all beings awaken to the light of their true nature. May all beings be free."

At the end of the minute, take a deep breath and know that you have been in communion with countless others all focusing their intent on the greatest good for all.

Golden Rule:

Do unto others as you would have them do unto you. So important is this idea, and so integral to the functioning of humankind, that it appears in all religious and philosophical systems as a basic tenet. We each must strive to be our best self and then reach out to the best self in others, treating them with compassion, empathy, kindness, and love. When we put another's well-being equal to or even, in times of need, above our own, we are adhering to a universal call to respect our own spirit self and the spirit self of others. The Golden Rule keeps us from harming another and, instead, encourages us to act only for the greatest good of all. Mindfully walking through our day, cognizant that others share our path with us and that they require the same love and nurturing that we do, will help to support a world dedicated to peace.

Core Strength for Peace

As we develop spiritual core strength, as we develop our internal energy core, we are able to share in each other's joys and sorrows, magnifying the former and alleviating the latter. When we are able to do this, we experience empathy, and in empathy are the seeds of peace. When we understand the joys and sorrows of others, we are more likely to avoid confrontation and instead pursue peace and compassion. Our ability to find and develop peace in ourselves, then, can be practiced in any setting, and in any environment, and we can allow this to expand beyond our immediate space and time and into the larger world.

We are all energy. The Namaste Response connects our energy—when we bring our energies together, anything is possible. When two or more are gathered with the same intent, anything is possible. Invention comes from tapping our energy into the greater energy—inspiration = breathing this in. All is energy, all energy is connected—we are then one!

About the Author

Tobie Hewitt holds an MFA in Creative Writing from Brooklyn College, where she studied poetry with Allen Ginsberg. She is an accomplished wordsmith whose work has appeared in a variety of large and small local, regional, and national publications. She has taught college-level English courses, including "Perspectives from Outside of the Box," which examines works of magical realism.

Core Strength for Peace presents ideas on how to acknowledge and strengthen one's inner energy center to achieve a more peaceful and harmonious internal, home, work, and world environment. Through instruction and exercises, readers will become aware of tools they can utilize to cope with otherwise stressful situations in their life. Tobie is available for presentations that promote spiritual core strength.

Please visit her website, www.tobiehewitt.com, for information and links to her current projects and contact information to schedule presentations.

Made in the USA
Lexington, KY
12 December 2011